anythink

D0824427

# PIRANHAS

## — BUILT FOR THE HUNT —

by Tammy Gagne

Consultant: Dr. Jackie Gai, DVM
Wildlife Veterinarian

CAPSTONE PRESS
a capstone imprint

First Facts are published by Capstone Press,
1710 Roe Crest Drive, North Mankato, Minnesota 56003
www.mycapstone.com

**Library of Congress Cataloging-in-Publication Data**
Gagne, Tammy, author.
Piranhas : built for the hunt / by Tammy Gagne.
pages cm.—(First facts. Predator profiles)
Audience: Ages 6-9.
Audience: K to grade 3.
Summary: "Describes the features, behaviors, and adaptations that make piranhas skilled
predators"—Provided by publisher.
Includes bibliographical references and index.
ISBN 978-1-4914-8840-9 (library binding)
ISBN 978-1-4914-8843-0 (eBook PDF)
1. Piranhas—Juvenile literature. 2. Predation (Biology)—Juvenile literature. I. Title.
QL638.C5G34 2016
597'.48—dc23                                                    2015020221

**Editorial Credits**
Carrie Braulick Sheely, editor; Sarah Bennett and Juliette Peters, designers;
Tracy Cummins, media researcher; Tori Abraham, production specialist

**Photo Credits**
Getty Images: DEA/C. BEVILACQUA/De Agostini, Cover, Paul Zahl, 21, Raphael
GAILLARDE/Gamma-Rapho, 6, Tony Allen, 4-5; Minden Pictures: Pete Oxford, 13; Newscom:
Gerard LACZ/NHPA/Photoshot, 17; Shutterstock: Bonita R. Cheshier, 1, guentermanaus, 3,
Hayati Kayhan, 7, Maxim Tupikov, 2, pieropoma, Cover Back, Tina Rencelj, 20, underworld,
18-19, Yellowj, 9; Thinkstock: Jupiterimages, 11, pablographix, 15

Printed and bound in China.

007479LEOS16

# TABLE OF CONTENTS

# EATEN ALIVE!

One moment the water is quiet and still. The next it bubbles as hungry piranhas attack another fish in a **frenzy**. The fish had swum too close to a rough rock, cutting itself. As soon as the piranhas smelled the blood, they attacked their victim.

## FACT
Between 30 and 60 piranha **species** live in the river systems and other **freshwaters** of South America.

**frenzy**—a wild or disorderly activity

**species**—a group of animals with similar features

**freshwater**—water that does not have salt; most ponds, rivers, lakes, and streams are freshwater

# HUNTING HABITS

Piranhas live in groups called **shoals**. But the fish do not always work together when hunting. One piranha will attack smaller **prey** on its own. Piranhas will go after a larger animal all at once. These attacks are usually fast and disorganized.

### FACT

A group of hungry piranhas can strip the meat off prey surprisingly quickly. In some cases nothing is left but bones just a few minutes later.

**shoal**—a large group of fish

**prey**—an animal hunted by another animal for food

# SURPRISE ATTACKS

Piranhas **ambush** prey. Hiding allows them to watch other fish without being noticed. One second the piranhas might be hiding in underwater plants. The next, they can be on the attack.

## FACT

When attacking their prey, red-bellied piranhas bite the animal's eyes and tail first. Both moves are quick ways to **disable** the other animal.

**ambush**—to make a surprise attack

**disable**—to make the body unable to work normally

# CUTTING THEIR MEAT

Piranhas have razor-sharp teeth, shaped like blades. Both the upper and lower jaws have a single layer of teeth. When the **predator** closes its mouth, the two rows interlock. This design is perfect for tearing flesh off prey.

## FACT
South American fishermen sometimes save the teeth of piranhas they catch. The sharp teeth are useful for making tools and weapons.

**predator** an animal that hunts other animals for food

# APPLYING PRESSURE

A piranha's powerful jaws **clamp** down on prey. The largest piranha species is the black piranha. Its jaws can apply 72 pounds (33 kilograms) of pressure on prey. This is equal to about 30 times the piranha's own weight!

## FACT

A black piranha's bite is three times stronger than that of an American alligator of the same size.

**clamp**—to hold or press together tightly

black piranha

# SENSING PREY

Piranhas have poor eyesight. But they have excellent senses of smell and hearing.

Piranhas also have special sensors along the sides of their bodies. The sensors pick up on movement in the water that can alert piranhas to nearby prey.

## FACT

Piranhas can smell blood from up to 2 miles (3.2 kilometers) away.

# EATING THEIR OWN

Piranhas will do whatever it takes to fill their bellies. When food is hard to find, they may even act as **cannibals**. Sometimes during a feeding frenzy, piranhas will bite one another accidentally. When this happens, any injured fish are likely to become a meal for the others.

## FACT

Piranhas often make a barking noise when fighting over food. They make the noises to scare off the other fish.

**cannibal**—an animal that eats its own kind

# SAFETY IN NUMBERS

Piranhas live in large groups for protection from predators. The largest species measure up to 13 inches (33 centimeters) long and weigh as much as 8 pounds (3.6 kg). Larger fish can eat a piranha whole. But predators may not bother attacking an entire shoal.

## FACT

Scientists have discovered that piranhas living in small groups breathe faster than those in larger ones. The researchers think this behavior could be a sign of fear.

# AT THEIR MOST DANGEROUS

Piranhas become especially dangerous when water levels are low. With less space they fight over prey. As food becomes limited, piranhas attack larger prey. Although it's rare, they may even attack people. These toothy fish are among the world's most powerful predators.

Piranhas often lay their eggs near underwater plants.

## AMAZING BUT TRUE!

Piranhas protect their eggs just as fiercely as they attack. A female can lay more than 5,000 eggs at a time. Both the males and females then swim back and forth to protect the eggs. The percentage of eggs that hatch is at least 90 percent. This survival rate is much greater than it is for other types of fish.

The water bubbles up as piranhas attack a dead capybara.

# GLOSSARY

**ambush** (AM-bush)—to make a surprise attack

**cannibal** (KAN-uh-buhl)—an animal that eats its own kind

**disable** (dis-AY-buhl)—to make the body unable to work normally

**frenzy** (FREN-zee)—a wild or disorderly activity

**freshwater** (FRESH-wo-tur)—water that does not have salt; most ponds, rivers, lakes, and streams are freshwater; oceans are saltwater

**clamp** (KLAMP)—to hold or press together tightly

**predator** (PRED-uh-ter)—an animal that hunts other animals for food

**prey** (PRAY)—an animal hunted by another animal for food

**shoal** (SHOHL)—a large group of fish

**species** (SPEE-sheez)—a group of animals with similar features

# READ MORE

**Gish, Melissa.** *Piranhas*. Living Wild. Mankato, Minn.: Creative Paperbacks, 2013.

**Hamilton, S.L.** *Piranha*. Minneapolis: ABDO Pub. Co., 2014.

**Niver, Heather Moore.** *20 Fun Facts About Piranhas*. Fun Fact File: Fierce Fish!. New York: Gareth Stevens Pub., 2013.

# INTERNET SITES

FactHound offers a safe, fun way to find Internet sites related to this book. All of the sites on FactHound have been researched by our staff.

Here's all you do:

Visit *www.facthound.com*

Type in this code: 9781491488409

Super-cool stuff!

Check out projects, games and lots more at
**www.capstonekids.com**

# CRITICAL THINKING USING THE COMMON CORE

1. Describe a piranha's teeth. How do the teeth help a piranha attack prey? (Key Ideas and Details)

2. Explain the piranha's ambush attack style. Using online or other print sources, find another animal that ambushes prey. Describe how the attack styles of the piranha and the other animal are the same and how they are different. (Integration of Knowledge and Ideas)

# INDEX